Hippos

by Conrad J. Storad

Lerner Publications Company • Minneapolis

For Eli, my first grandson
Always respect nature's creatures.

*The photographs in this book are used with permission of: PhotoDisc Royalty Free by Getty
Images, pp. 4, 39; © Richard G. Fisher/Root Resources, pp. 6, 21, 23, 38, 40; © James P.
Rowan, pp. 7, 8, 9, 13, 18, 19, 22, 24, 28, 41; © Michele Burgess, pp. 10, 11, 12, 15, 20, 25,
26, 27, 29, 30, 35, 36, 37, 42, 43; © Kenneth W. Fink/Root Resources, pp. 14, 16, 17;
© Bruno Vincent/Getty Images, p. 31; © Robert Gill; Papilio/CORBIS, p. 32; © Joe McDonald/
CORBIS, p. 33; © Peter Davey/Bruce Coleman, Inc., p. 34; © Royalty-Free/CORBIS, pp. 46–47.
The map on page 5 is by Laura Westlund.
Cover: © Royalty-Free/CORBIS*

Lerner Publications Company
A division of Lerner Publishing Group
241 First Avenue North
Minneapolis, Minnesota 55401 U.S.A.

Website address: www.lernerbooks.com

Library of Congress Cataloging-in-Publication Data

Storad, Conrad J.
    Hippos / by Conrad J. Storad.
        p.   cm. — (Early bird nature books)
    Includes index.
    ISBN-13: 978–0-8225–2869–2 (lib. bdg. : alk. paper)
    ISBN-10: 0–8225–2869–X (lib. bdg. : alk. paper)
    1. Hippopotamus—Juvenile literature. I. Title. II. Series.
  QL737.U57S766 2006
  599.63′5—dc22   2005007474

Manufactured in the United States of America
1 2 3 4 5 6 – JR – 11 10 09 08 07 06

Contents

Hippos live in many parts of Africa. The striped areas show where most hippos live.

Be a Word Detective

Can you find these words as you read about the hippo's life? Be a detective and try to figure out what they mean. You can turn to the glossary on page 46 for help.

blubber   endangered   herds
bristles   extinct   mammals
bull   gaping   nostrils
calf   habitats   territories
cows   herbivores

Chapter 1

Hippo *is short for*
hippopotamus.
How did the hippo
get its name?

The Hippo

The river flows slowly. The water sparkles in the light of the setting sun. Suddenly there is a *whooooooshing* sound, then a loud snort. A huge head appears out of the water. It's a hippo, one of the largest animals on Earth.

Hippo is short for hippopotamus. *Hippopotamus* comes from a Greek word that means "river horse." The hippo got its name because it spends so much time in the water.

Hippos spend most of the day wallowing in rivers and lakes.

There are two different kinds of hippos. They are the pygmy [PIHG-mee] hippo and the river hippo. The pygmy hippo is very rare. It lives along streams and swamps in the rain forests of western Africa. A pygmy hippo is about 5 feet long. It can weigh as much as 600 pounds.

This is a pygmy hippo. The pigmy hippo's scientific name is Hexaprotodon liberiensis.

This is a river hippo. The river hippo's scientific name is Hippopotamus amphibius.

The river hippo is much more common. River hippos are giants. A male river hippo can weigh up to 8,000 pounds. That's heavier than two small pickup trucks stacked on top of one another! Let's take a look at the river hippo.

Hippos have bristles of hair on their faces.

River hippos are mammals. Mammals are animals that feed their babies milk. All mammals have some hair on their bodies. Some mammals are very hairy. Other mammals have hardly any hair at all.

Hippos do not have much hair. They have just a few bristles on the front of their faces. They also have tiny hairs inside their ears and on the tips of their tails.

Hippos live in central, eastern, western, and southern Africa. They live in places with lots of water nearby. Hippos live by swamps, lakes, and slow-moving rivers. The places where hippos live are called habitats (HAB-uh-tats).

These hippos are wading through a swamp in Kenya.

Hippos look clumsy on land. But they are like big ballerinas in the water. Hippos have thin webs of skin between their toes. This skin helps them move through water easily. Hippos move underwater in a slow-motion gallop. Their toes barely touch as they dance along the bottom of a lake or river.

Hippos seem very clumsy. But they move gracefully in deep water.

Hippos make snorting sounds when they come to the water's surface.

Hippos can stay underwater for up to five minutes. But they usually come to the surface every minute or so for fresh air. A hippo's ears close when the animal sinks underwater. Its nostrils close too. Nostrils are the breathing holes on a hippo's nose. When a hippo comes to the water's surface, it breathes out through its nostrils with loud snorts.

Hippos often rest with their heads peeking out of the water.

An adult hippo has a large head. It has big eyes and small nostrils. The hippo's eyes and nostrils are high on its head. So are its tiny, round ears. Even when most of the hippo is underwater, its eyes, nostrils, and ears can be above the water's surface. Hippos can see, breathe, and hear when they are floating in water.

The hippo has a huge mouth. A hippo's mouth can open about 4 feet wide from top to bottom. Most first graders could stand up inside a hippo's mouth when it is open all the way!

Hippos can open their mouths very wide.

Hippos show off four sharp teeth when they open their mouths. The two biggest teeth on the bottom are long and thick. A male hippo's bottom teeth are up to 20 inches long.

Four of a hippo's teeth are large and sharp.

These hippos are resting in the sun. When it gets hot outside, a hippo's skin makes a pinkish red liquid. The liquid protects the animal from the sun.

Hippos live in sunny places where it gets very hot. But hippos have ways to protect themselves from the sun. Hippos' skin makes an oily, pinkish red liquid. The liquid keeps the hippos from getting sunburned. It also helps keep the hippos' skin from getting too dry.

17

Hippos have smooth, thick skin. Below the skin is a layer of fat called blubber. The blubber helps the hippo stay warm when it is in cool water. The blubber also helps the hippo float. Without it, the hippo might sink to the bottom like a big rock.

A hippo has smooth skin. There is a thick layer of blubber underneath the skin.

Chapter 2

Hippos eat grass. At what time do hippos eat?

Feeding Time

Many animals sleep when the sun goes down. But sunset is not a time to rest for hippos. Nighttime is when hippos eat.

Hippos use their lips to tear off grass. They eat large bunches of grass.

Hippos are herbivores (HUR-buh-vorz). Herbivores are animals that eat only plants. Hippos eat a lot of grass. Hippos don't nibble grass with their teeth. They tear off the grass with their wide, tough lips. Then they swallow large clumps.

Hippos eat grasses that grow along rivers and lakes. They eat all night long. They eat up to 100 pounds of grass every night! Hippos also drink more than 50 gallons of water every day.

Hippos are big animals. So they need to eat a lot.

Hippos will walk for miles to find grass to eat. But they never get too far from the water. At sunrise, they head back to the rivers and lakes. It's time for hippos to rest and cool off.

When the sun comes up, hippos go back to the water to rest. They spend all day in or near the water.

Chapter 3

This is a group of hippos. What is a group of hippos called?

Life in the Herd

Hippos live in groups called herds. A herd is usually made up of 10 to 15 hippos. But herds can be as large as 100 animals.

Herds of hippos keep cool during the day in lakes or rivers.

One large male hippo leads the herd. A male hippo is called a bull. Female hippos and their babies are members of the herd. Female hippos are called cows. The herd also includes a few young bulls.

Herds live in home areas called territories. Herd leaders do not want hippos from outside the herd to come into their territory. The leader will fight any male hippo that challenges him in his territory.

A bull will defend his territory. This hippo was hurt in a fight with another animal.

If a bull gets too close to another bull's territory, the herd leader gives a warning. He snorts loudly and then opens his mouth wide. He shows off his teeth. This is called gaping (GAYP-ing). The other bull may decide to leave. Or he may choose to fight. Then the bulls run at one another. They slash each other with their huge teeth.

These hippos are fighting in the water.

Markings help hippos find their way to grassy places.

Bull hippos mark their territory so that other bulls won't come near. They mark their territory by spraying it with urine and droppings. The markings tell other hippos that they should stay away. Markings also are like road signs for members of the herd. They lead the way from the water to grassy feeding areas on land.

Hippos use lots of sounds to talk to members of their herd.

Hippos also tell one another things by making different noises. Hippos are usually quiet when they are on land. But they make lots of sounds in and under the water. Hippos make a honking sound to call to one another. When one hippo calls, other members of the herd usually answer.

Hippos usually call out early in the morning. They call out again at sunset.

Hippos also grunt and growl. They even scream. Scientists don't know for sure why hippos make all of these noises.

Scientists are studying hippo sounds. They want to find out what each different sound means.

Chapter 4

This is a baby hippo with its mother. What is a baby hippo called?

Mothers and Babies

Mother hippos usually give birth in the spring and fall. Mother hippos have only one baby at a time. A baby hippo is called a calf. Young hippos live near their mothers until they are about 8 years old.

Mother hippos go to quiet places to have babies. They often give birth in shallow spots in lakes or rivers. Sometimes baby hippos are born underwater. The calf rises quickly to the surface to take its first breath. Newborn baby hippos are bright pink.

Baby hippos play in the water right away.

Baby hippos are very big. They are almost 3 feet long at birth. They weigh between 60 and 100 pounds.

A calf can swim and walk just minutes after it is born. But it must stay close to its mother. Calves drink their mothers' milk. Baby hippos need lots of milk so they can grow.

Mother hippos take care of their babies.

Hippos eat many different kinds of grass.

The calf grows fast. It can gain more than 1 pound a day. After about eight months, the baby hippo learns to eat grass.

A hippopotamus calf stays with its mother.

Mother hippos keep their babies safe. They watch their calves closely. A baby hippo walks close to its mother's neck. That way, the mother hippo can see her baby.

In the water, a baby hippo must swim close to its mother's side. If the mother stops, the calf must stop. Sometimes the mother hippo leaves the water to find some grass to eat. Then the baby walks just behind her.

Lions and crocodiles hunt baby hippos. But mother hippos are fierce fighters. Their jaws are powerful enough to bite a crocodile in half!

This is a crocodile. Mother hippos are strong enough to protect their babies from crocodiles.

Baby hippos walk in line behind their mothers and place themselves according to age. The youngest follows closest to its mother. The oldest brother or sister follows at the end of the line.

A baby hippo follows its mother wherever she goes.

Young hippos stay close to the herd.

A young hippo does not leave its mother's side until it is two years old. Then it begins to do some things on its own. But the young hippo always stays close to the herd. Hippos start their own families when they are about nine years old.

There is not as much land for hippos as there once was. What is happening to the land where hippos live?

The Future for Hippos

You can see hippos at many zoos in the United States. But it is getting harder to see hippos in the wild areas of Africa. More and more people are moving into the areas where hippos live. There are few places left for the hippos to go.

Some people hunt hippos. Many hunters want hippo teeth. The hunters make money by selling the teeth. Others hunt hippos because the big animals eat farmers' crops.

Hippo teeth are made of ivory. Ivory is very valuable.

There are fewer than 200,000 wild hippos left in Africa. Someday hippos may become endangered. An endangered animal is an animal that might die out forever. Some kinds of wild hippos have already died out forever. Animals that have died out forever are extinct.

Hippos may become endangered.

It is fun to learn about hippos.

Scientists want to learn how to keep hippos safe. They study how hippos live. Learning about hippos is important.

Many zoos have hippos that you can visit.

You can learn about hippos too. There are lots of ways for you to learn about hippos. Visit a zoo and watch them. Or go to the library. Read about hippos and other animals that live in Africa. By learning about hippos, you can help make sure that these amazing animals stay around for years to come.

Have you ever seen a hippo?

On Sharing a Book

As you know, adults greatly influence a child's attitude toward reading. When a child sees you read, or when you share a book with a child, you're sending a message that reading is important. Show the child that reading a book together is important to you. Find a comfortable, quiet place. Turn off the television and limit other distractions, such as telephone calls.

Be prepared to start slowly. Take turns reading parts of this book. Stop and talk about what you're reading. Talk about the photographs. You may find that much of the shared time is spent discussing just a few pages. This discussion time is valuable for both of you, so don't move through the book too quickly. If the child begins to lose interest, stop reading. Continue sharing the book at another time. When you do pick up the book again, be sure to revisit the parts you have already read. Most importantly, enjoy the book!

Be a Vocabulary Detective

You will find a word list on page 5. Words selected for this list are important to the understanding of the topic of this book. Encourage the child to be a word detective and search for the words as you read the book together. Talk about what the words mean and how they are used in the sentence. Do any of these words have more than one meaning? You will find these words defined in a glossary on page 46.

What about Questions?

Use questions to make sure the child understands the information in this book. Here are some suggestions:

What did this paragraph tell us? What does this picture show? What do you think we'll learn about next? Where do hippos live? Could a hippo live in your backyard? Why/Why not? How do hippos talk to each other? What is their favorite food? How much do hippos eat each day? What do hippos do during the daytime? What are baby hippos called? What do you think it's like being a hippo? What is your favorite part of the book? Why?

If the child has questions, don't hesitate to respond with questions of your own, such as What do *you* think? Why? What is it that you don't know? If the child can't remember certain facts, turn to the index.

44

Introducing the Index

The index is an important learning tool. It helps readers get information quickly without searching throughout the whole book. Turn to the index on page 47. Choose an entry, such as *herds*, and ask the child to use the index to find out how many hippos are in a herd. Repeat this exercise with as many entries as you like. Ask the child to point out the differences between an index and a glossary. (The index helps readers find information quickly, while the glossary tells readers what words mean.)

Where in the World?

Many plants and animals found in the Early Bird Nature Books series live in parts of the world other than the United States. Encourage the child to find the places mentioned in this book on a world map or globe. Take time to talk about climate, terrain, and how you might live in such places.

All the World in Metric!

Although our monetary system is in metric units (based on multiples of 10), the United States is one of the few countries in the world that does not use the metric system of measurement. Here are some conversion activities you and the child can do using a calculator:

WHEN YOU KNOW:	MULTIPLY BY:	TO FIND:
miles	1.609	kilometers
feet	0.3048	meters
inches	2.54	centimeters
gallons	3.785	liters
tons	0.907	metric tons
pounds	0.454	kilograms

Activities

Imagine that you are a hippo. What would you do in the daytime? At night? Make up a story about it. Draw or paint pictures to go with your story.

Baby hippos grow fast. If you grew as fast as a baby hippo, how much would you weigh in one month? In six months? In one year?

Hippos eat lots and lots of food. What if you ate like a hippo? What would you eat every day?

Glossary

blubber: a layer of fat under the skin

bristles: short, stiff hairs. Hippos have bristles on their faces.

bull: a male hippo

calf: a baby hippo

cows: female hippos

endangered: in danger of dying out

extinct: gone forever

gaping (GAYP-ing): opening the mouth wide

habitats (HAB-uh-tats): the areas where a certain kind of animal can live and grow

herbivores (HUR-buh-vorz): animals that eat only plants

herds: groups of hippos

mammals: animals that feed their babies milk and have hair on their bodies

nostrils: holes to breathe through. Hippos have nostrils on their noses.

territories: animals' home places

Index

Pages listed in **bold** type refer to photographs.

About the Author

Conrad J. Storad grew up in Barberton, Ohio. He works at Arizona State University, where he is the editor for two nationally award-winning magazines, *ASU Research* and *Chain Reaction*. He also is the author of 17 science and nature books for children and young adults, including *Saguaro Cactus, Scorpions, Tarantulas, The Circulatory System,* and *Inside AIDS: HIV Attacks the Immune System*. Conrad lives in Tempe, Arizona, with his wife, Laurie, and their miniature long-haired dachshund, Sophia. Together they enjoy trout fishing, hiking, and exploring the wilds of Arizona and the Southwest.